The Penny Drops

An Eazi Pezi guide to investing in small business

By

L A Watson

Published in 2016 by L A Watson

All images, text, ideas and content are the property of Larissa Watson.

Contact details for permissions, rights and royalties via
lw.creativeconsult@gmail.com

Copyright © 2016 by Larissa A Watson

Contents

Forward

Introduction

1   The Penny slot

2   Why? Motivations and directions

3   Experience of your market

4   Energy, money, resources

5   Value

6   Input to output

7   Timing

8   Stability

9   Buyer Beware

10   Legal & Intellectual Property

Glossary

Resources

Forward

I love businesses, small, medium and large but especially small companies. There is something so exciting and real in watching people take an idea and developing it into a business that grows to become a living growing machine. I have always been interested in the mechanics of how this happens, in the steps taken and the environmental factors that determine the outcomes achieved. Whether the outcomes are purely organic growth or that which is process and strategy driven in nature can depend on a variety of factors and this simple guide will cover some of the insights and observations I have had the opportunity to discover. My experience is based both in running my own companies and in teaching, consulting and researching other businesses over the period of twenty-five years.

This is a very simple guide to investing in companies, it will provide you with the pertinent questions to ask, and the key base issues to explore if you are looking at the viability of buying into or over a working company or investing in a new business concern.

Who is this piece aimed at?

This collection of observations and insights is a combination of theory and practical experience and is aimed at those who may be interested in starting their own company, buying into an existing company as an executive or non-executive director or first time Angel investors. It will assist those wishing to research the likely viability of certain business models, sectoral peculiarities, business types and management teams. The book is short because it is designed to be read and digested in an afternoon so that you can develop an objective overview of the proposed business and likely return on investment and length of term required to harvest that investment.

I believe that if start up entrepreneurs evaluated their own potential businesses in a cold clinical detached manner the way an investor would then they might make very different decisions moving forward!

∞

Introduction

On a sunny day in July last year I found myself returning from an early morning meeting in Derry which is seventy or so miles from home, Belfast, and as it was a beautiful sunny morning I uncharacteristically took a detour off the main road and found myself in the nearby seaside resort of Portrush. I bought myself a guilty pleasure lunch of a curry chip which I ate with a plastic fork while I sat and watched families playing on the beach. Then I walked up the main street and found myself in the institution which is Barry's Amusements. Barry's Amusements has stood for generations and as a child we would have spent some rainy summer holidays playing on the penny slots and messing around on the bumper cars with friends.

The amusements were quiet on that Thursday. As the sun shone outside, the hall of penny slots sang with the rattles and tunes of machines calling only to each other with flashing lights and dancing illuminations. I walked aimlessly through and as I stopped, I glanced at the pile of shrapnel change I'd dug out of my purse and then proceeded to weed out the coppers with which to 'play'.

When I was a kid we would save our pocket money up for weeks before the holidays. One year I made the mistake of spending all my savings in the first couple of hours of the first day by getting carried away at the amusements. I went off to complain to my parents, I suppose I was looking for sympathy or to be furnished with more cash but I was treated to a wry laugh from my father and "that'll teach you to throw your money away into those machines". I was not a happy girl, did learn my lesson though and it was years before I could walk inside an arcade again.

I since learned that the only money you should gamble with is that which you can afford to lose. I feel this way about unproven or under researched business investments.

One never plans or intends to lose money though, so in a very simple way I have laid out some of the pertinent questions and considerations that might provide the potential investor with some foresight and understanding of how return on investment might be more clearly defined in assessing a business proposition.

∞

The Penny drops

As I stood and fed my coppers into the slot machine, one by one, like in a trance I watched the mechanics and watched the coins. They dropped down through the cogs and lights, then landed onto the slider piled high with coins, waiting for the slider to slowly move back and fro, pushing the creeping bank of coins forward and back until some would teeter over the edge and fall out the shoot.

I thought.... This little penny slot machine is just like a business. It's just like the process of investing money in...movement of energy/product or service...money out, and watching the mechanics I became amused at all the parallels of this micro mechanism to the mechanics of the macro business process.

Let me explain,

If you look at one of the coin drop machines you can see that there is a downward drop to input money, we will call this the investment input, a moving plate onto which the coins drop, this we will call the project or product and a second tray to hold all the coins that are pushed forward, this is the company overhead and structure and some of these eventually shift forward and fall off the end into the outward shoot, the return on investment or ROI.

How to decide if you should play can depend on the cost to 'play', the value of pay-out, the stability of the fund, the time and money required to invest before any ROI is likely to happen and your motivation for 'playing'' in the first place.

∞

2. Why?

The most important question you can ask yourself or your co-investors is, WHY, why invest, Why this company and why this product at this time?

Are you looking for another income stream? A project, is this to be your sole income? I Would advise a thorough examination whatever your motivations as it is important to know what you want out of the venture. This will inform and guide your decision making.

Then look at the proposition Why this company, why this sector and why this product or service?

Is there a need for this product or service – having a market need or requirement is very often the biggest indicator of venture success.

Where is your point of pain?

I trained as a designer, in this area we were taught to look for the 'point of pain'. Simply put, the 'point of pain' is the part of a product, service or user experience that annoys you the user to the point of pain. In finding the point of pain the innovator or designer wants to change the process. In wanting to make an improvement one that will make a difference. This maybe is not even obvious in the first place but through innovating to introduce a new function, a new use or a redesign the process will vastly increase the user experience. The point of pain is often the place where we identify a new need or the requirement for a new product or service.

To assess the market need or requirement it helps to look at Maslow's theory of hierarchy of needs.

1. Biological and Physiological needs - air, food, drink, shelter, warmth, sex, sleep, etc.

2. Safety needs - protection from elements, security, order, law, limits, stability, etc.

3. Belongingness and Love needs - work group, family, affection, relationships, etc.

4. Esteem needs - self-esteem, achievement, mastery, Independence, status, dominance, prestige, managerial responsibility, etc.

5. Cognitive needs - knowledge, meaning, etc.

6. Aesthetic needs - appreciation and search for beauty, balance, form, etc.

7. Self-Actualization needs - realising personal potential, self-fulfilment, seeking personal growth and peak experiences.

(The original model developed in the 1950's had five levels but this was adapted in 1970's to include Cognitive needs and aesthetic needs)

In Maslow's model each of us is motivated by needs. Our most basic needs are inborn, having evolved over tens of thousands of years. The Hierarchy of Needs helps to explain how these needs motivate us all.

Maslow's Hierarchy of Needs states that we must satisfy each need in turn, starting with the first, which deals with the most obvious needs for survival itself.

Only when the lower order needs of physical and emotional well-being are satisfied are we concerned with the higher order needs of influence and personal development.

So, if the things that satisfy our lower order needs are taken away, concern about our higher order needs is less important.

This model can be used to explain how and why certain products do better than others and where they sit in the market or greater population.

This amended model shows how the theory can be applied to products and services:

Biological and Physiological needs - help-lines, social housing, security benefits, Samaritans, roadside recovery, AA, RAC.

Safety needs - home security products, burglar alarms, house and contents insurance, life insurance.

Belongingness and Love needs - dating and match-making services, chat-lines, clubs and membership societies, Mac Donald's, 'family' theme-parks.

Esteem needs – plastic surgery, cosmetics, fast cars, home improvements, furniture, fashion, shoes, clothes, drinks, lifestyle services.

Self-Actualization needs - Education; and spas, self-help manuals, only 2% of population are self-actualizers, so they don't constitute a very big part of the mainstream market.

Our amusement arcade and the penny slot machine fits into this model on two levels. The arcade is a place where friends and families hang out to spend time together so satisfying belongingness and love needs while the experience of playing the machines and gambling satisfies esteem needs where the individual through 'playing' can feel like a winner and experience heightened emotions through the drama of jeopardy.

∞

3. Experience of your Market

It does not matter if you are investing in your own business or an existing venture, having market knowledge about the sector you are working in is essential to success and will help you stay ahead of the pack.

Knowing something about the sector you are working in is essential to success and will help you stay ahead of the pack.

Your market includes your customers, your suppliers and your competitors. These three are pivotal characters that define the success of your business.

Your customers are the ones buying from your business. Get to know what they like, how much they will spend, what they enjoy and what they need will give you a better understanding of what they will want from you, enabling you to translate your product into something that will sell to your target market. In developing a product or service it's important to actually talk to your customers and ask them what they think. You should be influenced by what they will buy, not by what you think they need. Don't work on assumptions

Know the suppliers and the reps, as this is often a valuable source of unofficial industry information about new products, competitor's movements and upcoming projects.

A good place to start to evaluate your customer is by looking at your competitors. What are other people out there doing that is similar to your business? What are they doing well? What do your customers like and dislike about the competition? This will give you the insight needed into how to make your product or service even better on price and quality.

look at the industry generally and then study it to identify gaps where you can create value.

There will always be new competitors so it's important to keep your eye on the market as there is innovation within existing companies and new competitors starting up all the time. Keep your eye on what's going on, and how your customer's needs are changing. To stay ahead, you need to ensure you know everything that is going on in your market and have an intuitive feel for where developments are heading – leading from the front is the best way to ensure you're not being overtaken.

Sectors ripe for success

Investing in a new business or investing through buying into a going concern are two differing routes into business. There are new businesses popping up all the time but the harsh realities and statistics show a depressing 50 per cent of start-ups don't make it past their first year in business.

When buying a business, going for one that's already established can help to minimise risk – especially if you invest in a thriving industry. This can be done via buying into a franchise which provides a framework and well developed model, it is a way of reducing risk however it brings limitations in how you proceed and can be an expensive option. Here are five types of business that are good right now:

Hand car wash

The wash cars by hand industry has grown considerably in the past five to ten years. they have materialised at abandoned petrol stations and at your local supermarket.

Nearly any space can be utilised to setting up a car wash. There are few government regulations. The set up costs are low and the main overhead is rent and staff.

All that's needed is a water supply, equipment (buckets, chamois, detergents etc.) and capital for staffing costs.

The location is important to a car wash business and the best locations are always in sight of 'chimney pots' simply put this means, near to residential and shopping areas. When your customer can leave the car with you and do their shopping it allows for great time management and adds an additional sense of satisfaction.

Online business

Online is where most of our business is being done, so the devices we use and the networks we use to communicate, network, date and shop are all growing and lucrative markets with international application.

The evolution of technology and mobile communication means that you can now run a business from pretty much anywhere in the world and on nearly any device, so devices, applications and networks continue to be growth areas although the market is constantly changing and very congested.

Social media for businesses means that it's easier than ever to reach a wider audience at little or no cost.

Gaming, online game and virtual reality platforms are also a growing and lucrative market where smaller firms can make significant and impressive return on investment through sales, licensing and IP deals.

E-commerce is a growing global industry, and as more and more people opt to shop from the comfort of their own homes, online marketplaces are thriving.

According to E-consultancy.com and their figures from The Centre for Retail Research, UK online sales are predicted to reach circa 52 billion in the 2016-17 year (equating to 15 per cent of all retail sales in the UK).

Coffee shop

The Irish and British tea-obsession has morphed into an American and European trend that sees us becoming a nation of coffee fiends.

The coffee shop industry has seen 15 years of rapid expansion, has proven resilient in the face of the recession and still remains one of the most successful sectors in the UK economy.

The Telegraph reported last year that 'coffee shops are replacing pubs in Britain', becoming social venues and alternative workspaces.'

Director of Allegra strategies, Jeffrey Young believes that 'there are still thousands and thousands of places in the UK that don't yet have a decent coffee experience'.

Senior care

The number of people aged over 65 is expected to rise from 10.6 million in 2010 to 16.1 million in 2016' and according to the Financial Times the 'demand for care homes is already outstripping supply'.

The UK care sector has seen a wave of foreign investment in recent years, and despite the hefty overheads, investing in the care home industry can still be a lucrative investment.

The main attraction for buyers is the longer leases available for care homes circa 25-30 years compared to shorter leases for other types of commercial properties, which allow a long-term fixed income from rent or ongoing net profit.

Julian Evans, head of healthcare at property group Knight Frank, says "last year the market was particularly 'hot' and that care home investments can be highly profitable, offering annual returns of 10 per cent or more – and the opportunity for capital growth."

Restaurants

The UK dining market is worth over £40 billion according to PwC. Restaurants are a popular option for potential buyers as even in turbulent economic times people will still eat out although different sectors and regions will experience different degrees of profit margin.

Like independent coffee shops, the market is not yet saturated and there is still plenty of space for smaller independent businesses and niche markets.

The competition is tough, although restauranteurs who want to stand out from the rest can enjoy success with niche products and options like food trucks, an organic, traceable menu, speciality, health and delivery options.

Foodie culture, street food trucks and the pop up phenomenon have greatly benefitted this sector. Now an industry in its own right pop-ups are worth 2.1 billion to the UK economy, meaning that there are now more ways to market your restaurant than ever before and making it a great time to get involved.

"Adapted from Melanie Luff, Business for sale"

∞

4. Money, Energy, Resources

When we walk past the penny drop machines we often see massive piles of coins ready to tip and assume that these will be an easy take. Much in the same way that we might look at a long established company, or a business that has already done mammoth research and development and seems ready to output revenue but a closer look at these situations is always necessary.

This question goes back to resources and evaluating the total value of the company in terms of fixed costs to keep it running and also in terms of the market value of the output of the product or service offering that is proposed. A question of costs and economics, does the total value of the company capital costs and fixed costs equate with a genuine return on investment when the production and research and development costs are balanced?

The financial aspects of investing in a business whether it be your own or another's are probably the most important to get right.

I believe that if start up entrepreneurs evaluated their potential businesses in a cold clinical detached manner the way an investor would then they might make very different decisions moving forward!

Cash Flow

When you are standing in front of the penny slot machine 'playing' the game it is essential that you have enough of the correct coins to keep playing until you have an output. This is your cash flow. It takes time to go away to get cash and then find a kiosk or machine to change currency. These processes will take you away from your game so it is important to correctly judge how much you will need before you start so that you are able to continue 'playing' until the first outputs start arriving. This is why a cash flow forecast is very important, it keeps you 'in the game'.

Overhead

Over head or company structure, we need to look at this in terms of how much does it cost to run the company, as in fixed costs before you invest or before a product or project begins. Is this cost effective, are the right staff in place, are these staff qualified and cost effective in terms of what they can promise and what they can bring to the table in expertise, experience and enthusiasm. Good people cost money but do you have the right combination of talent and financial responsibility on board. Only you can make this call but you have to trust that the company is based on industry knowledge and expertise and is equipped accordingly.

Are the premises cost effective and fit for purpose?

You need to decide if you are looking at an overhead heavy business or if the returns justify the premises and staff involved in bringing the proposed product or service to market. Very often companies invest heavily in an infrastructure that is before their market competency and beyond their true worth in an effort to win market favour and investor approval. In my view (and this is a personal view brought about through observation and experience) a company which chooses to influence through cosmetic means has usually extended themselves in ways that often do not manufacture significant returns to justify the market image generated, however, this is a fine balancing act and staff costs, rent and rates should be evaluated to get a true picture of the story against current clients and net revenue before making a judgement.

∞

5. Value

Value of company resources and outputs in relation to market forces.

In the penny slot analogy this relates to the amount of cash you have to invest into a company to get a significant return on investment. As in, is the company overhead heavy? Is the project going to generate enough return revenue to justify the investment required to move the project along?

You need to research the market for the product or service the company will generate for you and decide if it is a marketing function or a sales and costs function that will bring you return on investment. This will encompass an assessment of the sales and marketing functions in addition to an honest and accurate overview of the market for the proposed product in the markets you aim to sell in. If you propose to extend the market for the proposed product or service, please check if there has been preliminary research done in prospect markets and what the results were before making assumptions. There are great trade bodies and maybe even competitor companies throughout the UK and Ireland who have done exploratory market research into alternative European and International markets who will help with preliminary information in these regards. Don't write off paying for research as it is often a cheaper alternative in the long run.

Valuation of business

There are two common formulae for the valuation of a business, the discounted cash flow technique and the multiples technique. Most sectors of business have a formula for valuing the business based on multiples of net profits, accountants can usually provide the multiple for your sector.

If the multiple is, for example, five times net profit, then the value calculation is simple.

It is very important to bear in mind that the selling price is what someone is willing to pay for the business at a specific time.

So what can you do to build equity and increase the multiplier?

When you develop a strategic plan to build the business assets you can increase the multiplier in a number of ways.

An owner-run business can ask for a higher multiple when there are staff who are able to run the business when the owner is not there. When the business is not dependent on the owner, it is more valuable.

If the business has a unique system that sets it apart from the competition, that increases the multiplier further.

The business is capable of bringing substantial new product ranges to market.

The ability to create new distribution channels that bring new clients to the business.

The business creates a strong brand that affects everything about the business, the multiplier increases still further.

The multiplier peaks when the business proves that it is scalable and could be rolled out nationally.

∞

6. Input to Output

How far the point of input is to the point of output

When I watched the coins trickling down the slot, landing and being pushed through the process of return a pertinent thought that struck me.

This is your money and your money and it's in there for the duration of the process.

This in reality means that you have to wait until the entire process runs its course, probably more than once and most likely a number of years to get any return on investment.

With this in mind, you are putting your money away for a certain and often uncertain amount of time and you have to be happy with this.

Certain company business models look to a five-year exit strategy for investors, others in new product development look at longer. A new company often is trying to get an investor to fund part of the research and development cost and sales and marketing operations, they then pay ongoing dividends from the net profits based on sales performance. You have to be somewhat happy to forget about the investment until or if it comes good. How long is this process? Are you happy with the time and finance investment because if you are also involved as an executive or non-executive investor director. In some industries it is easy to assess the term of an investment like film or TV because these industries are very time based but in an industrial based sector it may take more time to recover your input. You have to be both patient and specific in terms of sector and term about your investment. How are you going to take your exit if it works and if it does not, where are you left? This is why you need good legal guidance from an experienced business firm.

∞

7. Timing

Timing of financial or resource input is crucial and directly correlates to the output.

If you are investing in a specific project or product launch, then the timing of investment in projects should be strategically measured in terms of the length of time it takes to produce output x twice so that planning is focused. You want to make sure that there is enough time and resources in place to ensure your project is correctly resourced and the end results are supported with enough time, staff and money to ensure success. You should check that all preparation costs are covered, the required staff are enlisted and if appropriate marketing resources are covered in terms of staff, advertising, design and time allocated in a timely manner. If appropriate seek out tax credits for research and development costs or research tokens tendered against university facilities. These take time to access and implement so ensure adequate time provision and if necessary amend expectations accordingly (for example, add six to nine months to the schedule although it may take longer) Materials and resources should be deployed effectively at the right stages of the project so that it has the best chance of creating a strong impact and return on investment. When adequate time and planning is deployed to operations then success in ventures is facilitated, shortcuts in marketing, sales and necessary resources will impact negatively on your project success.

The need to strategically time resource input to return investment is even more critical when the business resource reserve or overhead is larger and therefore the output return on investment needs to be larger to balance the books and keep the stakeholders happy.

∞

8. Stability

The stability of the company, how long has it been operating

When assessing the penny slots something that struck me was the mounds of coins held in reserve in the trays, it got me thinking about the stability of company structure and how important that a secure staff cohort was. If you don't have the necessary skills, experience, longevity and strategic vision within the company structure then you will experience weakness and unplanned turbulence within the inner core of your investment. It is therefore important that the team in charge of your investment are both focused and dedicated to giving you return. Many small companies need investment but are no more interested in having investor responsibilities than vegans eating at the steak house. You need to ensure that the people who say they need and want your money will really work with and for you. This is a partnership and what works in January for both parties may not work in October, get to know the personalities, get references, get involved! If you are respectfully hands on they know you are there and will understand that you are there for the long term, investment is not a short term activity! If appropriate it is good for business to get involved even in an advisory role and attend regular management meetings to keep track of the project or product development.

The Team

turnover of staff will have a correlated impact on the lack of company stability. This is a very important factor in maintaining investor/management relations and successful return on investment is dependent on a stable long term management team is essential. This issue, however, can be sectoral specific especially relevant to the Creative Industries in terms of Film, TV and games/software design as many contributor's work freelance, this however can be addressed if the freelance team is an established, long-term arrangement whereby the same people or firms work together on a regular basis. This overcomes the need to spend time building new relationships, initiating new structures or procedures and therefore builds a team that ensures the stability of the company or project. These days freelance and sub-contract workers are becoming much of the norm as both recognise the benefits to the more flexible arrangements. Benefits to workers include; flexible working for those with families, the ability to work at home or at times that suit you, working on a number of interesting projects for different companies, a higher hourly or contract rate, choosing when and how much holiday time you want. Drawbacks include; having to manage your own NIC, taxes, VAT and pension arrangements and no sick pay or holiday pay. For the employer the benefits include; being able to keep overheads tight and employing contract staff on an 'as required' basis, managing resources more effectively, not having to maintain facilities for as many resident staff, able to pick and choose creative and expert talent on a job by job basis, happier more content staff also tend to work harder and more creatively, although the negatives can be that you may not always have the personnel you want when you want as they may be otherwise contracted, you will pay higher hourly rates and have less control over work output.

∞

9. Buyer Beware!

The one thing this analogy does not cover but which is clearly very important is that of studying any existing company accounts and sales records. In the analogy we take it that we don't have access to historical company records and pay outs but some research of the market and through the present owners and companies house should furnish these. The importance of the work above mentioned cannot be underestimated as it is easy for a company to misrepresent their current and historical standing in terms of income and revenue. I know of many people who were both new and experienced business professionals who have been caught buying into and over existing businesses. These have been expensive mistakes and have led to pensions and cash windfalls being misplaced. Buyer Beware!

When it's all over

If you followed the guidance above and 'played' a good game, then you will have brought insight and wisdom to your choices. You are not the frustrated punter kicking the machine or wringing their hands, no, you are a winner because either you made a handsome return on your investment, or, because you took precautions legally and contractually and were you not comfortable about how things were going, you knew when to walk away with your bank balance and dignity intact.

∞

10. Legal

Lawyers

Law practise is diverse and finding a good general business lawyer is essential. Ideally this should happen before you are in the position to require legal services. Ask around for recommendations and do your research on various firms before deciding on one. You will be looking for a firm that handles a number of firms of your size and preferably in your sector so that they have experience and knowledge of the particular issues that might arise. Certain legal areas are specialised and you may only appoint representation as and when required, for instance in intellectual property or patent law. These specialists may not operate in your area or region so be prepared to travel to get someone with the requisite experience. Legal work is expensive and can be painstakingly slow so it is important to get the most experienced and relevant advice and representation possible. I had experience to get involved in a trade mark issue a couple of years ago and to fight my case I had to get two separate 'expert' lawyers on the case. In the end the case was settled to my satisfaction, not through any work of the lawyers but through my own background research and negotiations.

Structure of the business

Initial questions regarding your business structure will examine the legal entity. Setting up a limited company in which you, your business partners and any investors can hold shares, is the usual and sensible option. A limited company has the key advantage of limiting personal liability of the owners of the company. Your company will have a separate 'legal personality', and can borrow money and enter contracts in its own right.

The advantages of incorporating a company outweigh the limited administrative burden of running it, which includes annual returns, accounts and filings.

If you set up a company, it is very important to have a properly drafted shareholders' agreement which will protect each shareholder's investment and govern what happens with the shares in various circumstances such as buying out, dilution, selling on.

Other options include a limited liability partnership, but limited companies are the most popular and flexible.

Domain names and trade marks

Before choosing the name of your business you should carry out some basic online searches to avoid potentially problematic business names or duplication in different sectors or the availability of domain names, trademarks and to ensure that you will have free reign in regards to future business expansion or product development. You can carry out trade mark searches at the UK Intellectual Property Office. These searches take just a few minutes but can flag registered trademarks which are similar to or identical with your potential business name, and so reduce the risk of you inadvertently infringing other party trademarks.

You may choose to use your business name or your new product as your trade mark although businesses may choose only to invest in only once they have established themselves. Registering a company at Companies House means that no one else can register a company with that exact name, but it does not give you any 'trade mark-type' rights. It will not prevent others from using your company name as a trading name, or registering it as a trade mark. However, registering a trade mark means that you can prevent others from using the mark or similar marks to refer to the same kinds of goods or services.

Website and software development

If you use independent developers, make sure you review the terms of their contract carefully before agreeing to them. Deadlines that the developers are working towards should be set out clearly in writing, however, it is wise to allow time to run and test and review before sign off. You should not agree to pay the full developer's fees until you have the opportunity to properly road-test the software.

Developers will own copyright in code and content they create for you, unless you have a written agreement to the contrary. Whether or not there is written agreement addressing the copyright position, you will have (in almost all cases) an implied licence to use the code or content for the purposes for which it was created. In order to own the copyright, which has certain important advantages over merely having a licence, you need to have a written assignment of copyright signed by the developer and in some cases it is worth negotiating or paying for this if it is the basis of a new or unique product, process or concept.

Copyright and Third party material

In using third party material, such as music, video or text, you are being liable for copyright infringement unless you have a licence or written permission to use it for the purposes set out.

User-generated content can enhance a website or app, but poses a number of risks. The content could contain third party copyright material. If you allow the use of third party material on your website or app you can be liable for content even though you were not responsible for posting it. If you do allow user-generated content to be posted, you should have terms and conditions which prohibit uploading infringing, illegal or defamatory content, and you should make clear that you reserve the right to remove content at your discretion. There should also be a properly handled notice and take-down procedure in place, whereby anyone who objects to content can request that it is removed. A safety measure can be to ensure that all material used by your business is reviewed internally for possible infringements.

Cookies and personal data

Recently introduced regulations on cookies now mean provide that any website that uses cookies must give users information about their use on the site and the purpose.

In the collection of personal data, you must comply with the Data Protection Act (please see regional and national regulations in this regard). Most businesses will collect or use client data in some way so compliance and accountability are essential.

Intellectual property (IP)

Intellectual Property (IP) rights are the most valuable assets a business can have. They are the total and final results of intellectual and creative effort. In the effective commercialising and protecting of IP a business can enhance its value in the eyes of investors and financing institutions. It is therefore crucial that businesses firstly understand what they have and then adopt measures to protect against 'infringements', in other words another party exploiting, copying or otherwise using your IP rights without your authorisation.

Why IP matters

The importance of securing IP rights cannot be overstated although small firms are often lax about the protection of relevant brands, designs, music and inventions. IP rights however, are key intangible assets to any business and they can be used to leverage and encourage financing of the company to aid its growth, and its market value.

Holding registered IP rights will increase the perceived value of the business in attracting investment and financing for a company. It can make the difference between lending and not lending for some angel investors. Registered IP rights act as a form of insurance that the company holding those rights has achieved the freedom to use the rights and to prevent third parties from copying them.

In a business exit strategy for sale of the company, any prospective buyers will/should perform thorough due diligence exercises before purchase. A key part of this process is to determine the extent and value of any IP in the company for sale. If no registered IP is in place, the eventual value and purchase price of the company will undoubtedly be far lower. This is because there is a risk by buying a company who may actually be unaware they are infringing someone else's trade mark.

The Federation of Small Businesses (FSB) says small firms are struggling to protect the identity and ideas at the heart of their businesses, with a quarter of the businesses surveyed with intellectual property rights a quarter are suffering some sort of violation or infringement within the last five years.

Strategies that can be adopted to deter potential infringers are prominent marking of the protected article which communicates to the public that the IP right in question exists. This includes using the © followed by name and date, for trademarks you can use ® symbol to indicate that you have a registered mark, and for unregistered trademarks you can use the TM symbol. ACID is an organisation which aims to raise awareness of IP in design and it is worth joining if you are in the design field.

When an IP infringement occurs

A small company obviously does not have the same resources as a large plc and as costs involved in infringement litigation can be substantial there are some positions that can be taken before the situation gets before the courts.

Get legal advice as to whether infringement does in fact arise? If infringement does arise, the first step is to draw the infringer's attention to the infringement, by asking your solicitor to issue a cease and desist letter.

Very often upon receipt of the letter the infringer will cease their activities and perhaps agree to pay compensation to the IP right holder. Many IP disputes are resolved in this way, with settlement agreements being entered into to ensure that no further conflicts arise in the future.

If this does not work it may be necessary to escalate matters through bringing infringement proceedings before the courts. It is now possible to sue for infringement at the 'Intellectual Property Enterprise Court' (IPEC) at a lower cost than before the High Court and in some cases it is possible to use the small claims track at the IPEC.

The infringement in question might amount to a criminal offence that Trading Standards might wish to pursue or the UK Border Agency may be willing to take action if infringing products are being imported into the EU. If the infringement relates to a trademark, it might be possible to file a complaint at the Advertising Standards Authority.

The Intellectual Property Office are a valuable resource and run a mediation service which is a way of getting expert assistance without high costs, if you can get the infringer to agree to mediate.

Respect for and protection of your Intellectual property is essential for your business growth and success.

∞

In Conclusion

"In the business world, the rear view mirror is always clearer that the windshield."

I like this quote by Warren Buffet, and yes it would be wonderful to have a crystal ball or time machine. I therefore conclude with some nuggets of wisdom for your consideration.

I have undertaken some projects and ventures throughout my career that upon reflection have not been a resounding financial success. In fact, I have reflected on certain projects and concluded that I would have been better spending the money on a good holiday, however, I rarely lost money and always gained something. Review and assessment are important and in assessing the intangible benefits of a project and venture it is important to look at the experiential process, the learning curve, satisfaction and fulfilment that were achieved, the long term market and the brand profile development.

Very often the true financial outcomes or return on Investments come much later in unexpected guises, and through the people and companies that you have interacted with on your journey. It is therefore my opinion that we must act with complete integrity in all our dealings and enjoy the process in its entirety.

I have though come to the conclusion that we do indeed attract what we believe to be true, and have experienced this in both positive and negative instances. I have gone ahead in projects where I had pre-conceived expectations as to the outcomes and my expectations were in fact reflected in the final outcome. This has been, both in terms of profitability, and people that I partnered with. It would be difficult to say if this was the law of attraction at work or my intuition and experience, nevertheless, beliefs and expectations are a valid ingredient in the return on investment frequently experienced in all life's adventures.

So go ahead and lead by example, develop the people around you so that they may achieve their potential and, above all, follow your dreams with passion. For what are we here for if not to live, love and experience creating the world we want to live in, where we can aim for the stars and if by any chance we don't get there we will still have risen above our own expectations of what we can be.

∞

Glossary of Terms

Administrator Insolvency practitioner appointed by the court under an administration order, by a floating charge holder, or by the company or its directors filing the requisite notice at court.

Board of directors A body responsible to the shareholders for the running of a company.

Business Industrial, commercial or professional services entity established to supply products and/or services to its customers.

Business angel A high net individual who wishes to invest in a start-up or fast growing businesses.

CEO Chief executive officer – usually the most senior executive director of the company and responsible to the board of directors for the running of the company.

Chairperson The chairman/chairperson of the board of directors of a company, responsible primarily for chairing meetings of the board. Usually this is a non-executive role or an executive position.

Company A business registered with Companies House

Creditor an individual or company owed money by another individual or company

Debt Money owed to an individual or company

Debtor an individual or company that owes money

Director A person who is appointed to the board of directors of a company. This may be an executive or non-executive role.

Dividend in a normal situation any payment distribution made by shareholders and paid out of profits. In an insolvency, any sum distributed to unsecured creditors.

Enterprise Value

This is the value attributed to a business and is calculated by taking the market share price by number of shares issued plus debt, less cash and investments. It is a measure of the real value of the company as a going enterprise.

Fixed charge A charge by banks or investors held over the company's fixed assets. The debtor cannot sell assets without the consent of the secured creditor or repaying the amount of the charge.

Floating charge A charge held over the general assets. The company may trade the assets (stock) without permission until the charge becomes fixed on appointment of an administration receiver.

Guarantee A written undertaking to pay a debt by a third party should the third party default on payment.

IP Intellectual property

IPEC Intellectual Property Enterprise Court

IPO Intellectual property office

Liquidator The official receiver or insolvency practitioner appointed to administer the liquidation of a company.

MBI Management buy in.

MBO Management buy out

Net present value (NPV) difference between the present value of cash in and cash out. Used to determine which projects are most attractive in a market or investment appraisal.

NICs   National insurance contributions

Official receiver   An officer of the court and civil servant employed by the insolvency service dealing with bankruptcies and compulsory liquidations.

Partnership   A contractual relationship between two or more people carrying on a joint business venture, each incurring liability of any losses, as well as the right to share profits.

Public limited company   A company with limited liability whose shares may be sold to the public. There must be £50,000 od issues shares before the company can trade.

PLC   Public Limited Company

Receivership   A company in administrative receivership.

Secured creditor   A creditor who holds security, such as a mortgage, over a person or company's assets for money owed.

Self-employed   A person who works for themselves and is not employed by another person or company so can work for more than one client.

Shareholder   The owner of one or more shares in a company.

SME   Small and medium enterprise.

Sole trader   A person working on their own account, who is self-employed, and is not registered as a company.

SWOT Strengths, weaknesses, opportunities, threats related to a company.

TS   Trading Standards

VAT   Value added tax. A sales tax applied to companies or individuals trading at or above the set rate of turnover. This varies in different EU states and across different products and sectors.

Venture capital

Capital investments in a company, which may be high risk investment, with potentially significant gains if the valuation of the company increases rapidly following the investment.

Voluntary liquidation   Method of liquidation not involving the courts.

∞

Resources

Useful websites

Institute of Directors	www.iod.com
Lawyers	infolaw.co.uk
Accountants	icaewfirms.co.uk
Venture Capital	www.bvca.co.uk
Business Angels	www.nban.co.uk
London	www.lbangels.co.uk
N Ireland	www.haloni.com
Federation of small business	www.fsb.org.uk
Chambers of Commerce	britishchambers.org.uk
Company news	ukbusinesspark.co.uk
Dun & Bradstreet	dbuk.dnb.com

Research

NOP	www.nop.co.uk
MORI	www.mori.com
UK Trade and Investment	uktradeinvest.gov.uk
Office for National Statistics	statistics.gov.uk
European Information Centres	euro-info.org.uk
British market research	bmra.org.uk
Research Buyers Guide	rbg.org.uk

| International research | esomar.org |
| Organisations | worldopinion.com |

Business Links

England	www.businesslink.gov.uk
Wales	www.businesseye.org.uk
Scotland	www.bgateway.com
Northern Ireland	www.investni.com
London	www.business4london.co.uk

Business statistics

Companies house	www.companieshouse.gov.uk
Small business service	www.sbs.gov.uk
Insolvency	www.r3.org.uk

Business Websites

www.is4profit.com

www.businessgo.co.uk

www.smallbusiness.co.uk

www.newbusiness.co.uk

Design

Design council	designdirectory.org
DTI Best Practice	dti.gov.uk/bestpractice
UK patent Office	ukpats.org.uk
British Library Patents	bl.uk/patents

Funding

DTI Research & development   dti.gov.uk/crd

Grants for businesses gov.uk/ regionalinvestment

R&D tax credits - www.dti.gov.uk/rd-guide/rd-taxcredit.htm

Grants for new ideas   dti.gov.uk/innovative-idea

Small firms loan   dti.gov.uk/sflg

Science and tech   nesta.org.uk

Collaborative research   ost.gov.uk/link

Princes Trust   princes-trust.org.uk

Government Departments

Inland revenue   hmrc.gov.uk

VAT   hmrc.gov.uk

DTI   dti.gov.uk

Patent office   patent.gov.uk

∞

Made in United States
Orlando, FL
11 May 2022